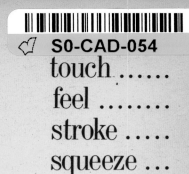

touch ......

feel ....

stroke .....

squeeze ...

The Art of Erotic Massage

Here, at last, is a book that can do more for your
sex life than all other "sex manuals" combined.
Written for the layman, THE ART OF EROTIC
MASSAGE will show you how your fingers,
hands, and mouth can become penultimate
instruments of pleasure.

Every part of the body is covered, with special
techniques for each area diagramed and
explained. The art of self-massage for relaxation
and conditioning is included, along with advice
on how to work with various creams and lotions
as developed by Masters and Johnson.

THE ART OF EROTIC MASSAGE is an extra-
ordinary book that can teach anyone how to turn
every inch of you, him, or her into an erogenous
zone . . . how to make every touch turn into new
ways of sexual fulfillment.

SIGNET Titles of Related Interest

The Art of Erotic Massage

by Stanley Whelan, Ph.D.
and Rachel Cochran

A SIGNET BOOK from
NEW AMERICAN LIBRARY
TIMES MIRROR

SIGNET TRADEMARK REG. U.S. PAT. OFF. AND FOREIGN COUNTRIES
REGISTERED TRADEMARK—MARCA REGISTRADA
HECHO EN CHICAGO, U.S.A.

SIGNET, SIGNET CLASSICS, SIGNETTE, MENTOR and PLUME BOOKS
are published by The New American Library, Inc.,
1301 Avenue of the Americas, New York, New York 10019

First Printing, July, 1972

PRINTED IN THE UNITED STATES OF AMERICA

To B<small>RIAN</small> R<small>ICHARD</small> B<small>OYLAN</small> *from both of us*

Contents

1. How Massage Can Improve Your Sex Life 13

What Is Massage? 14
Massage and Health 14
Massage and Sex 15
Should You Attempt Therapeutic Massage? 16
How Frequently Should Massage Be Performed? 17

2. The Perfect Massage 19

Time 20
Place 21
Circumstances 22

3. Preparing and Caring For Your Hands 25

Limbering Up 27
Developing Manual Sensitivity 27
Strengthening Your Fingers and Grip 29

4. Diagrams of the Areas of Massage 33

5. Techniques of Massage 37

Petrissage 38
Judo Chop Technique 40
Circular Vibrating Technique 43
Consecutive Fingertip Maneuver 44
Fingertip Stroking 46
Fingernail Stroking 47

6. Massaging the Different Parts of the Body   49

Head   53
Face   53
Neck and Shoulders   55
Back   60
Arms   66
Legs and Buttocks   69
Chest and Breasts   74
Abdomen   77
Ano-Perineal Region   80
Male Genitals   83
Female Genitals   86
Oral Massage   88

7. Massage with Vibrators and Other Appliances   89

Vibrators   90
Whirlpools   94
Shower Spray   95
Electric Toothbrush   95
A Few Devices to Keep Away From   96

8. Massage with Creams and Lotions   99

9. Self-Massage   103

Whole-Body Relaxing Massage   104
Facial Conditioning Massage   107

10. Japanese Massage   109

11. Swedish Massage   *115*

    Effleurage   *116*
    Vibration   *117*
    Sauna and Steam Baths   *117*
    Massage with Willow Branches   *118*
    Massage with Palm Leaves   *119*
    Hot and Cold Towels   *120*

12. Massage during Coitus   *123*

    Penile Massage during Coitus   *124*
    Massage of the Female Breasts and
      Genitals during Coitus   *125*
    Anal and Other Extragenital Stimulation   *126*

The Art
of Erotic Massage

1

How Massage
Can Improve Your
Sex Life

PEOPLE like having their bodies touched. It is pleasant, relaxing, reassuring, and if properly done, sexually stimulating.

Touching a person's body in a sexually stimulating way is nothing less than an art: the art of erotic massage.

This book will teach you how to give one.

What Is Massage?

Massage may be defined as the application of tactile pressure for a given effect. The intended effect might be:

1. Therapy; that is, relief of pain or cure of a particular ailment;
2. General bodily conditioning;
3. Relaxation;
4. Sensual gratification;
5. Sexual arousal and/or gratification.

One massage, of course, may serve several of these purposes.

Massage and Health

The therapeutic benefits of massage are well documented. By skillfully manipulating muscles and joints, masseurs and masseuses have successfully treated paralysis, muscular atrophy, sprains, contractions, chronic and subacute afflictions of the joints, local venous congestion, obesity, constipation, sciatica and other neuralgias, headaches, and a host of other ailments.

Here's how the treatment works:

While tissues are being massaged and shortly afterwards, a greater than usual quantity of blood flows through them. The number of red corpuscles increases, and it is believed that the hemoglobin value of the corpuscles increases also. At the same time, the flow of the lymph stream is accelerated.

This physiological activity has several consequences. First, unhealthy cells and other products of fatigue are removed from the massaged tissues. Second, serous fluids — the serumlike liquids surrounding the tissues — are dispersed. Third, secretion and excretion are stimulated. Fourth, local and general cell nutrition is improved.

Not surprisingly, afflictions involving the muscles or joints respond well to such therapy. Likewise, healthy muscles are made stronger — just as they are in active forms of exercise — and the person being massaged enjoys overall bodily relaxation as well as relaxation of the individual massaged muscles.

Massage and Sex

Muscular relaxation is important sexually, for if a person isn't physically relaxed, he won't enjoy sex fully.

Tension makes the body physically less receptive

to sensation. It also distracts the mind from the pleasurable stimuli that are being received during sex play. Massage, by dissolving tension, removes these dual barriers to sexual satisfaction.

It also trains the body to be sexually more responsive. Many scientists believe that the more receptive the body is to sensual pleasure of any sort, the more receptive it will be to erotic pleasure. Massage increases general sensual awareness and thus schools the body to respond more keenly to sexual stimulation.

Should You Attempt Therapeutic Massage?

Therapeutic massage is a sophisticated procedure which requires a knowledge of anatomy and physiology far more extensive than can be communicated in a book of this size.

The reader, therefore, would be unwise to attempt to treat muscular injuries, sprains, or other ailments with the techniques he has learned here. In fact, such attempts at amateur therapy may aggravate the condition you are trying to cure.

Therefore, if you have an ailment that lends itself to the therapy of massage, consult a professional masseur or masseuse, a chiropractor, or a physician.

However, there is no reason why the attentive reader, with a little practice, should not be able to give a very good relaxing or conditioning massage or to employ massage techniques aimed specifically at sexual arousal and/or gratification.

The recommended approach is:

1. Read the book cover to cover, studying the dia-

grams and making sure that you thoroughly understand one section before going on to the next.

2. Reread the sections describing techniques that you plan to employ.

3. Practice the techniques on yourself when possible, and on others.

4. Incorporate your new knowledge of massage into your sex life.

How Frequently Should Massage Be Performed?

Most authorities feel that once a week is enough for whole-body relaxing and conditioning massage. Greater frequency, however, will not hurt and will often pay surprising sexual dividends.

If your partner is tense, irritated or anxious, whole-body massage may be just the thing he or she needs to put him or her in the mood for lovemaking.

First use the general conditioning techniques to relax your partner. Then go on to the erotic techniques for arousal and gratification.

These erotic techniques, of course, can be used independently of the relaxing and conditioning techniques. In fact, once you've learned them, you'll almost certainly employ some of them in every sex act.

Note: In the following instructions and illustrations, for the sake of clarity and convenience, the person giving the massage will be referred to as "M" and the person receiving it as "R."

2

---

*The Perfect
Massage*

A GOOD, satisfying massage—erotic or nonerotic—can be given just about anywhere, at just about any time, and under just about any circumstances.

But the best, most satisfying massages—erotic and nonerotic—are those that take advantage of time, place, and circumstance.

The more of these factors that you arrange to have working for you, the closer you'll come to the ideal of the perfect massage.

Time

Time of day is relatively unimportant when giving a massage, but timing the massage with R's (the recipient's) other activities can be important.

The worst time for receiving a massage is immediately after eating. The blood required for digestion is drawn from other parts of the body, and if M (the masseur or masseuse) is competing for it, both the massage and digestion will suffer. (Incidentally, for the same reason the worst time for sex is immediately after a meal.)

Another bad time for massage is immediately before a meal. Energy levels are low at this time, and massage consumes energy.

Other bad times are immediately after R has had vigorous physical exercise, when R is sleepy, and when R is not in the mood (the recipient must be able to relax if massage is to be helpful).

Virtually any other time is a good time, and some times are super-good.

A few of the super-good:

1. After a long, lazy day on the beach or in some other setting where energy consumption is low.

2. After a steam or sauna bath, especially if the bath is followed by a cold shower (the best of all possible times for massage).

3. After an evening at the movies, watching television, or engaged in some other sedentary pursuit.

4. When R is harried, tense, or anxious (extensive whole-body massage will relax him physically and put him into the mood for erotic massage and sexual intercourse).

5. After a hard day of mental toil, business pressure, et cetera, again use whole-body massage extensively to set the stage for sex.

Place

There are several obvious requirements for erotic massage: privacy, comfort, and lack of distraction.

A nonprivate place, open to sudden interruptions, is unlikely to lead to complete relaxation. Likewise, such distractions as a blaring radio or phonograph or a noxious odor are undesirable. However, bear in mind that some people become sexually aroused when they listen to certain types of music, and the more loudly it is played, the more exciting it becomes. Know your recipient's tastes.

Since it is essential that the place where massage is

performed permits M free access to R's body, be sure that your quarters are spacious and comfortable.

Ideally, relaxing and conditioning massage is performed on a professional massage table. This table can be adjusted to make it possible for M, while in a standing position, to work on any part of R's body.

If you don't have a massage table or some piece of furniture that can be made to serve as one, use a bed or the floor. Kneel or squat alongside R while massaging limbs, head, and face; straddle the torso while massaging it.

The room in which massage is performed should be warm, because muscles contract when the body is cold. An ideal temperature is seventy-five degrees.

During summer months relaxing and conditioning massage may be performed outdoors, but at temperatures below sixty degrees the enterprise won't be very successful.

Circumstances

Skillfully performed at the right time and in the right place, a massage is already close to perfection. To push it across the finish line, attempt to adjust circumstances so that:

1. None of the other four senses is being stimulated in a way that interferes with R's appreciation of tactile stimulation;

2. Stimuli to the other four senses enhance, whenever possible, R's tactile enjoyment.

To illustrate: No one, with the possible exception of the president of a tobacco company, can relax fully in a room filled with stale cigarette smoke. Other unpleasant odors can be equally discomforting.

Therefore, whenever possible, air a room thoroughly before massaging in it. If you are feeling adventurous, you might also want to light a burner filled with a mild and fragrant incense. No strong scent should be used, however; the purpose of the aroma is not to distract but to contribute to R's feeling of complete relaxation.

Bright lights are conducive to neither relaxation nor erotic stimulation. The curtains or shades in the massage room should be drawn during the day, and night lighting should be kept fairly dim.

To control completely the light level in your room, use a rheostat. These devices fit into the socket that houses a standard light switch and may be purchased at any hardware store for about five dollars.

If you don't use a rheostat, substitute a colored bulb for the standard one now in your lamp. Colored light can create an exciting and erotic effect even in the most prosaic of rooms.

There is not much you can do to provide stimulation to the taste buds in a way that will enhance R's enjoyment of massage; in fact, taste sensations generally overpower tactile sensation.

However, you can prevent ungratified taste longings from being distracting. Give R a mint, a small glass of grapefruit juice, or something similarly unfilling yet with a strong, distinctive taste. (This will be especially important if R is dieting.)

As for auditory stimulation, remember that loud noise of any sort is usually distracting. Paradoxically, total silence can also be distracting.

Ideally, your massage room will have a moderate level of what auditory engineers call "white noise" — the hum of an air conditioner or ventilator, the gentle rustle of wind outside the window, or soft and bland music on a radio or phonograph.

Probably the best background sounds for massage, especially for erotic massage, are rain on the roof, surf, or the burbling of a nearby stream.

However, *De gustibus non est disputandum:* There is no disputing tastes. A well-known stage actor claims that no sound is as relaxing, reassuring, and gratifying to him as that of sustained applause.

Finally, the tactile stimulation of massage should be enhanced by the pleasant feel of a comfortable massage table or bed. If a bed is used, a good, firm mattress and freshly laundered sheets will contribute to R's enjoyment. A nice added touch is to keep a sweet-smelling sachet in your linen closet.

You'll find more hints on ways to enhance massage in future chapters.

3

---

*Preparing and Caring
For Your Hands*

Even the most accomplished pianist will sound bad on a piano that is out of tune. The most skilled architect cannot turn out accurate blueprints with a faulty slide rule. Likewise, no masseur or masseuse can give a truly satisfying massage unless his or her hands are in good condition.

Rough, chapped, or calloused hands will chafe or irritate a partner's skin. Ragged or overly long nails can scratch or nick.

To keep your hands in the best possible shape, observe these rules:

1. Protect your hands at all times. If you must immerse them for any length of time in water or other liquids, wear rubber gloves. Also, wear appropriate gloves when gardening, doing carpentry or other work involving the hands, and during cold weather.

2. When you wash your hands, use a mild soap. If you have a dry skin, use soap containing cold cream or some other moisturizing ingredient.

3. After washing your hands, dry them thoroughly. Then protect and pamper them with a cream or lotion. (Select one that does not contain alcohol or other harsh ingredients.)

4. Keep your nails medium-short. Clip them regularly, and go over them with an emery board to keep them smooth.

Limbering Up

Limber up your hands by performing these two simple exercises immediately before giving a massage:

1. Clench your fists as tightly as possible. Count to five. Now unclench your fists, and stretch your fingers wide apart. Repeat this exercise ten times.

2. Let your wrists go limp. Shake your hands rapidly back and forth until your wrists feel absolutely limber and free. (It should take thirty to sixty seconds of shaking.)

Developing Manual Sensitivity

All the preparation in the world will be of no use if your partner is made to feel like a piece of meat that you, the butcher, are trying to tenderize. The key to a perfect massage is touch.

To increase your manual sensitivity, perform the following exercises:

1. Assemble a number of household objects which differ greatly in size, shape, and texture: for example, a glass jar, a small cutting board, a furry slipper, a piece of pumice stone, a sheet of paper, a tablespoon, a ball of wool.

Place the objects on a table. Sitting at the table, close your eyes, and pick up one of the objects. Touch the object as if trying to memorize every tactile detail of it, the way a blind person would with an object never before encountered. Note its shape, its size, and its texture. Think about what it feels like and what qualities you would look for if you were to identify it by touch in the future.

After examining the object tactilely for at least a minute, put it down, and examine another object. Continue until you have examined all the objects on the table. Then, still sitting at the table with your eyes closed, mentally review the objects, and try to re-create in your memory the feel of each one. If there is an object the feel of which you can't remember, go back and examine it again.

Perform this exercise every night for at least a week. If you're really ambitious, make it harder for yourself each time by choosing objects more and more alike.

2. Investigate the sensations of touching yourself in different ways.

Place your hands behind your head, with three

FIGURE 1

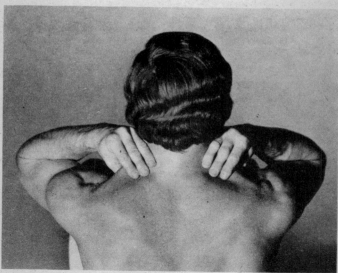

fingers of each hand on the upper part of each trapezius muscle (see figure 1 bottom of page 28). Using the circular vibrating technique (see Chapter 5), massage this muscle from the base of the skull to the farthest point downward that you can reach.

Experiment with different degrees of pressure. First be extremely gentle. Does your touch feel relaxing? Or is it too light to really take out the kinks?

Now exert fairly heavy pressure. Do you feel relief from tension? Or is your touch so heavy that its painful?

Practice this and all the other techniques described in Chapter 5. Study the different ways you can touch yourself and the way each type of touching feels.

Strengthening Your Fingers and Grip

None of the massage techniques described in this book will require greater strength in the fingers or in the grip than the average person possesses.

However, if your fingers or grip is weaker than average, here are two exercises with which you can strengthen them:

1. For the fingers: Fingertip push-ups (see figures 2 and 3).

Get in the standard push-up position — body prone, hands even with your shoulders, palms on the floor, weight supported on your palms and toes.

Now support your arms on your fingertips instead of your palms, and perform ten push-ups.

If you can't perform ten, perform as many as you can each day until your fingers are strong enough to support you for ten.

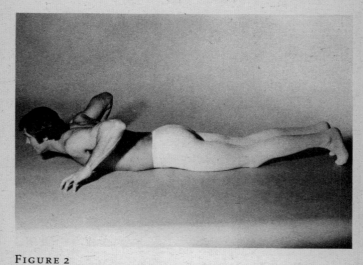

Figure 2

Figure 3

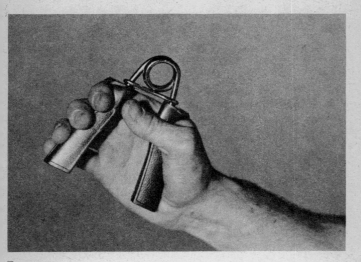

FIGURE 4

FIGURE 5

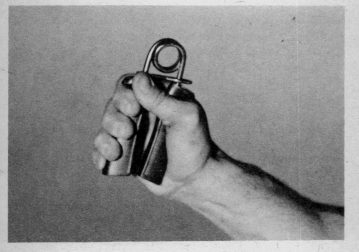

If you can perform ten without stopping in between, your fingers are strong enough; no need to continue the exercise.

2. For the grip: Squeezing (see figures 4 and 5).

Purchase a pair of nutcrackerlike gymnastic devices designed specifically for development of the grip. They can be obtained at any sporting-goods store and should not cost more than five dollars for the pair.

Practice squeezing them shut twenty-five times in rapid succession. If you can do it, your grip is strong enough for any demands that the techniques in this book will make upon it.

If you don't want to spend the money on these gymnastic devices, buy a hard rubber ball at any five-and-ten-cent store, and practice squeezing it until you can do so five hundred times without pausing.

4

Diagrams of the
Areas of Massage

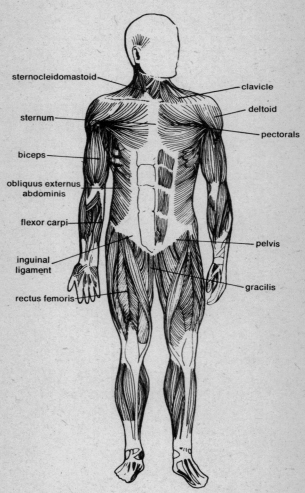

sternocleidomastoid

clavicle

sternum

deltoid

pectorals

biceps

obliquus externus
abdominis

flexor carpi

pelvis

inguinal
ligament

gracilis

rectus femoris

FIGURE 6: *Front View of the Human Body*

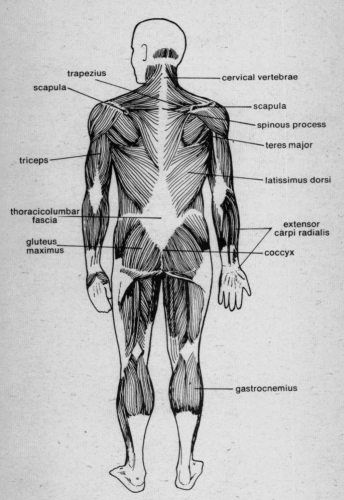

FIGURE 7: *Rear View of the Human Body*

Future chapters will refer to the various muscles and bones involved in massage by their scientific names. Before reading those chapters, familiarize yourself with the diagrams presented here.

It won't be necessary to memorize all the names in the diagrams. Simply look over the material, then mark this chapter with a bookmark so that you can quickly consult the relevant diagram when you come across an unfamiliar anatomical term.

5

Techniques of Massage

THE professional masseur or masseuse has literally hundreds of techniques in his or her repertoire, ranging from the violent twisting and jerking maneuvers of Japanese massage to the gentle, stroking motions practiced in certain refinements of Swedish massage. Brief familiarization descriptions of some of the more interesting of these techniques are given in Chapters 10 and 11.

However, for the types of massage that you will perform after reading this book, only six basic techniques are required: petrissage, the judo chop technique (tapotement), the circular vibrating technique, the consecutive fingertip maneuver, fingertip stroking, and fingernail stroking.

As you read the following descriptions of these techniques, practice performing them on yourself. The best part of the body on which to practice is the thigh; it is handiest, reasonably sensitive, and contains an adequate variety of muscles and surfaces.

Examples of how to adapt these techniques to different parts of the body will be given in Chapter 6.

Petrissage

Petrissage is a relaxing and conditioning technique drawn from Swedish massage (see figures 8 and 9).

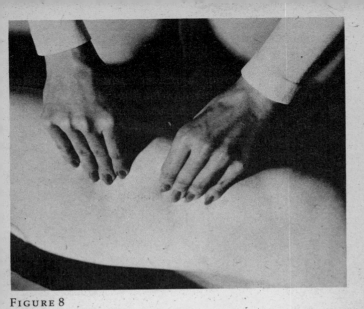

FIGURE 8

FIGURE 9

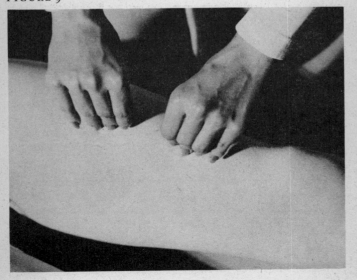

Grasp a substantial chunk of muscle between the fingers and thumb of both hands. Clutching the muscle firmly, lift it away from the underlying bone. As you lift, make a kneading movement with your fingers, permitting the muscle to slip through the fingers and return to its original position. At the conclusion of the movement your hands will be empty.

Now grasp another chunk of the muscle next to the one you just worked on, and repeat the maneuver. Continue until you've performed the maneuver on the entire muscle.

Petrissage is one of the best relaxing and conditioning techniques. It engorges the muscles with blood, strengthens them, and relaxes them.

It is most effective when performed on the large, thick muscles of the torso and the extremities—the trapezius, pectorals, latissimus dorsi, triceps, biceps, gluteus maximus, gracilis, rectus femoris, and gastrocnemius.

Its value in erotic massage is that it relaxes the body and thus prepares R to be more responsive to sexual pleasure.

Judo Chop Technique

This technique (see figures 10 and 11), is a staple of both Japanese and Swedish massage. In Swedish massage it's called tapotement.

Hold your hands straight out, the fingers stiff and on a plane with your palm, as if you were about to administer a judo chop.

Using both hands, alternately and very rapidly strike the area of the body being massaged. Start at

FIGURE 10

FIGURE 11

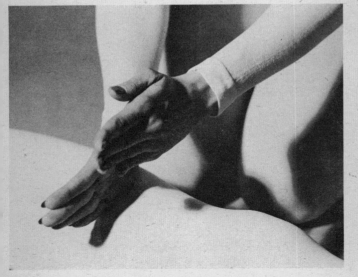

one end of a muscle and continue to the other, covering the entire area with brisk, firm blows.

The chops should land so close to each other that there is not any area of flesh that has not been struck. Think of the sides of your hands as being covered with ink, and pretend that you are trying to blacken completely the area being massaged.

Like petrissage, the judo chop technique is a relaxing and conditioning device. Its value in erotic massage is that it relaxes the body and thus prepares R to be more responsive to sexual pleasure.

In one variation favored by many Swedish masseurs and masseuses the area being massaged is struck with cupped palms instead of with the sides of the hands. This variation of tapotement shifts the balance of the scale slightly away from conditioning and toward relaxing.

The judo chop technique, with blows struck by the side of the hand, is especially effective in building the muscles of the abdomen. R lies on his back and lifts his feet about three inches off the floor, thereby tensing the abdominal muscles. M then vigorously pounds the entire abdominal area with a rain of judo chops—the harder, the better. (At the beginning of a program, of course, start moderately, and build up to more forceful blows.)

The judo chop technique, either with side-of-the-hand or cupped-palm blows, may also be used to condition and relax the pectorals, trapezius, latissimus dorsi, and other heavy muscles of the torso and extremities.

Do *not* use the technique on the face, neck, female breasts, male or female genitals, or other sensitive areas.

Circular Vibrating Technique

Far more gentle than petrissage or the judo chop technique, the circular vibrating technique (see figure 12), is still primarily a relaxer and conditioner, but it may also be used for direct sexual stimulation.

Place two, three, or four fingers on any part of the body. Pressing firmly against the flesh, make three or four circular movements. Do not lift the fingers off the flesh or rub them over the flesh. They remain in contact with the flesh at all times, and their movement causes the flesh and underlying muscles to move also.

FIGURE 12

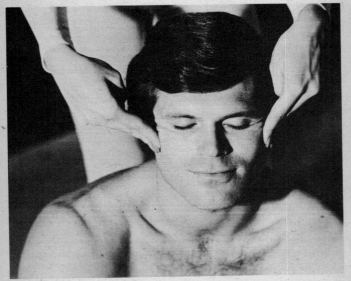

After performing three or four circular movements on the same area of flesh, reposition the fingers an inch away, and repeat. Continue in this manner until you have completely covered the area you wish to massage.

The circular vibrating technique is one of the most versatile massage techniques. It can be used to ease muscular tension, to cure headaches, to condition muscles, and to create sexual arousal. These various uses will be described in the following sections devoted to massaging the individual bodily parts.

Consecutive Fingertip Maneuver

The consecutive fingertip maneuver (see figures 13 and 14 is an exclusively erotic technique which can be used effectively on any part of the body. It is most effective on protuberant organs like the penis or the female breasts.

When employed on a flat surface of the body, the technique is as follows:

1. Hold the four fingers of one hand approximately half an inch above the body's surface.

2. Lower one finger at a time, letting it graze ever so lightly against the flesh, then raise it again. Start with the little finger, then the ring finger, then the middle finger, then the index finger, then the little finger again. As one finger leaves the flesh, another has just made contact; thus there is always one finger touching the flesh.

3. Continue, either with fingers touching the same area or ranging over a broader area, until the desired erotic effect is achieved.

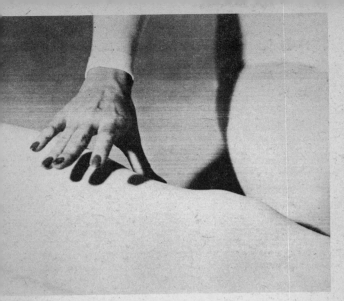

FIGURE 13

FIGURE 14

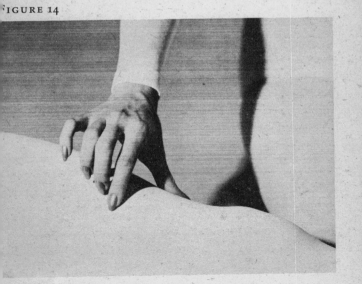

When employing the maneuver on a protuberant organ, take the organ in your palm and proceed to move the fingers as described above. (More specific instructions will be given in sections involving the individual parts of the body.)

Fingertip Stroking

Fingertip stroking is another maneuver employed solely for erotic purposes.

Apply the balls (tips) of all four fingers to any area of the body (see figure 15). As gently as possible, run the fingers across R's flesh. Ideally your touch will be

FIGURE 15

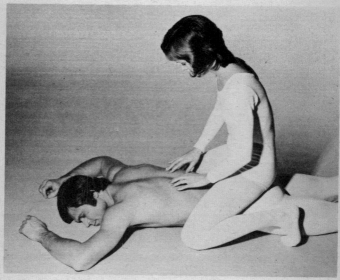

so light that R cannot identify the precise point at which you start or stop touching him.

Fingertip stroking is one of the most exciting techniques in erotic massage. It can be used with great effect on the genitals as well as on other parts of the body.

Practice it until you master it. Using your thigh or your face, experiment with different degrees of pressure.

If you get a tingly erotic sensation, you'll know you're doing things right. If this sensation does not come, your touch is probably too heavy.

Fingernail Stroking

Fingernail stroking is identical to fingertip stroking except that your fingernails rather than fingertips come into contact with R's body.

Do not overlook the importance of this technique. Though uncomplicated, it is one of the most exciting ways you can touch a person.

Practice it on yourself, experimenting with different degrees of pressure. As with fingertip stroking, a tingly erotic sensation is an indication that you're doing things right.

6

---

*Massaging the Different
Parts of the Body*

DIFFERENT PARTS of the body respond to touching in different ways. The caress that is exquisitely arousing when applied to the inner thigh may be sexually useless or even annoying when applied to the forearm. Likewise, the vigorous kneading that proves supremely relaxing when applied to the trapezius muscles can cause agonizing pain if applied to the female breasts.

Not all people respond the same way to the same touches; however, there is enough universality to their response that several ground rules can be drawn.

1. The face and throat are two of the most delicate parts of the body. Always massage them with a moderately to extremely light touch.

On athletic men the sternocleidomastoid muscle (see figure 6, p. 34)—the thick muscle running from the bottom of the ear to the collarbone on each side of the neck—is usually sturdy enough to withstand petrissage and occasionally the judo chop technique; but on most other people nothing more vigorous than the circular vibrating technique should be employed.

2. The muscles of the upper torso (see figure 6, p. 34)—the trapezius, deltoids, pectorals, latissimus dorsi—are extremely sturdy. Pressure exerted on them may be medium to very heavy, depending upon R's size and preference.

If R is slight of build or extremely sensitive, pressure should be light. Men as a rule can withstand considerably greater pressure than women, and athletic men considerably greater pressure than nonathletic men.

The female's pectoral muscles are, of course, part of her breasts; the female breasts should always be treated gently.

3. The abdominal muscles are among the strongest in the body and should be capable of withstanding virtually any pressure that the masseur or masseuse may apply. (Athletic men can frequently withstand punches to the abdomen delivered full strength. If, of course, an individual's abdominal muscles are weak, pressure must be adjusted accordingly.)

4. The limbs of an athletic person are normally capable of withstanding the same pressure as the muscles of the upper torso. The limbs of a nonathletic person must usually be treated fairly tenderly. On women the legs are frequently sturdier than the arms, whereas on men there is generally little difference.

5. The genital organs are extremely sensitive. Here the lightest touch will normally create the greatest excitement, whereas a heavy touch or even moderately firm touch may be painful. There is one significant exception: In most men the erect penis can be handled quite roughly. However, the testicles should always be handled gingerly. The female genitals should be accorded equal delicacy.

When you are massaging someone for the first time, frequently ask if you should press harder or more lightly. Learn your partner's particular preferences, and abide by them in future sessions.

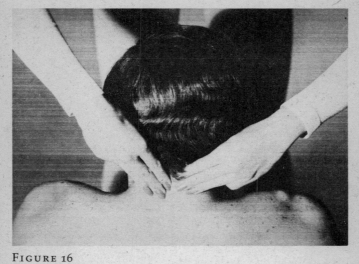

FIGURE 16

FIGURE 17

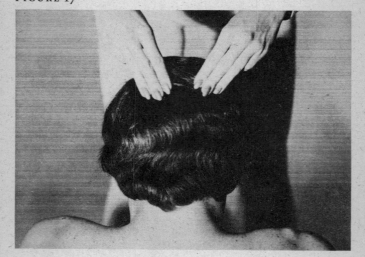

Now let us consider the individual parts of the body and the techniques that may be employed most effectively upon them.

Head

R sits, leaning against M. Using the circular vibrating technique, start at the rear hairline, and work your way to the top of the skull. Direct your pressure downward toward the neck. Continue to massage the entire head in this manner, following the pathways indicated in figures 16 and 17. Use especially firm pressure against the trapezius muscle; use light pressure on the sides of the head as you near the temples.

This massage will often relieve a headache stemming from nervous tension. In any case, the massage should prove relaxing.

There are no specific erotic techniques to be applied to the head; however, the relaxation that results from conventional head massage should increase R's receptivity to sexual arousal.

Face

Facial massage serves both relaxing and conditioning functions. A regular program of massage as described below should strengthen the facial muscles, giving them attractive firmness and tone; eliminate wrinkles; and relax the muscles in such a way that frown lines and other unattractive creases are diminished.

R lies on his or her back. M places the index and middle fingers of each hand on R's temples. Using the circular vibrating technique, M works fingers across the center of R's forehead until the fingers meet.

Continue to work horizontal paths across R's forehead until the entire surface, from eyebrows to hairline, has been covered. Then massage entire forehead again, using vertical paths. Begin at the bridge of the nose, and work your way straight up to the hairline; then, tracing parallel paths, work your way back to the temples.

Now R closes his eyes. Using the circular vibrating technique, run your fingertips over and around the eyes, exerting extremely light pressure toward the nose.

Next, massage the nose itself. Start at the bridge, and work your way downward, covering the entire nose. Use index and middle fingers and the circular vibrating technique.

Now, still employing these fingers and this technique, massage the area around each ear. Pressure should be light and exerted downward toward the throat.

Next, place the index and middle fingers of each hand on R's jawbone, directly below the ears. Using the circular vibrating technique, work your way toward the chin, where both hands will meet.

Proceeding similarly, trace parallel horizontal paths across the throat to the Adam's apple and across the cheeks to the lips and nose.

Now, continuing to use the circular vibrating technique but describing much larger circles, massage R's cheeks. The circular movement should cover the entire cheek, from jawbone to cheekbone, and should be made with all four fingers of each hand. Pressure is upward toward the temples.

Finish the facial massage by covering the entire face with light circular vibrating movements.

As with the head, there are no specific erotic techniques to be applied in facial massage; however, the relaxation that results should make R more receptive to sexual arousal.

Because of its excellent conditioning function, many people will want to perform facial massage upon themselves once or twice daily. Naturally, the above techniques can be adapted to self-massage (see Chapter 9).

Neck and Shoulders

The following three-stage massage is recommended for the front of the neck:

1. R lies on his back. M places the index and middle fingers of each hand just behind R's earlobes (see figure 18). Using the circular vibrating technique, firmly but gently work your way down the sternocleidomastoid muscles to the collarbone (see figures 19 and 20).

Now return to the top of the neck, this time placing your fingers just in front of the earlobes. Using the circular vibrating technique, trace two more paths to the collarbone—this time between the sternocleidomastoids and the Adam's apple.

Next, repeat the technique a third time, massaging the area just over the windpipe. Be sure to exert ex-

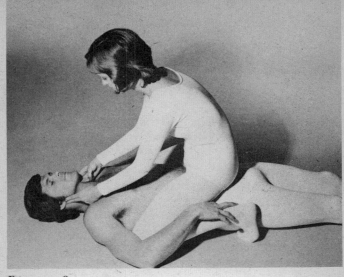

FIGURE 18

FIGURE 19

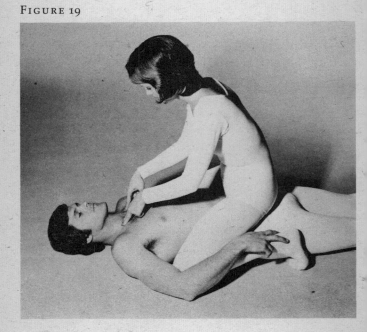

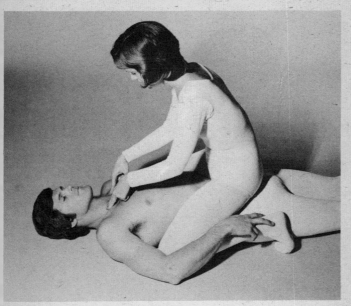

FIGURE 20

tremely light pressure; otherwise, you'll interfere with R's breathing.

2. Perform petrissage on the sternocleidomastoid muscles. Work on both muscles simultaneously or on one muscle at a time. Start at the collarbone, and work your way up to the skull, then retrace your route. Repeat until all tenseness has left the muscles or until R complains of weariness or pain. (If R's sternocleidomastoids are not fairly rugged, this step may have to be eliminated.)

3. Repeat the three maneuvers of Step 1 but in reverse order—first massaging the area over the windpipe, then the adjacent area, then the sternocleido-

mastoids. Remember, we have left petrissage and are now back to the circular vibrating technique.

After the front of the neck has been massaged, have R roll over onto his stomach. Massage the back of his neck, using the circular vibrating technique. Trace vertical paths from the hairline to the top of his spine. Pressure is firm and exerted downward toward the spine. Cover the entire neck, from sterno-cleidomastoid muscle on one side to sternocleido-mastoid muscle on the other.

If R is tense or nervous, the trapezius muscles will be very tight and will feel hard to M's touch. If this is the case, repeat the above massage several times, applying slightly harder pressure to increase blood flow. When you feel the muscles loosening up, per-form the exercise a final time, start to finish, with gentle movements. For this final time use very large circular strokes.

Either in conjunction with or independent of the above massage, you may employ petrissage on the trapezius muscles. Start where the muscles reach the skull, and continue downward to where they meet the scapulae (winglike bones of the back) (see figure 7, p. 35). The trapezius muscles are among the sturdiest in the body and should be able to with-stand vigorous petrissage, especially if R is athletic.

Either in conjunction with or independent of petrissage, you may also perform the judo chop technique.

To massage the shoulders, place one hand on each shoulder while R lies prone. Now raise and lower the shoulders in large circular patterns—first from the rear of the body to the front, then, after half a dozen repetitions, from front to rear. Pressure is exerted downward.

Repeat this maneuver until the shoulders feel loose and extremely mobile or until R complains of weariness or pain.

Now cover the entire shoulder area—deltoid muscles, lower trapezius muscles, and teres major muscles (see figures 6 and 7)—with the circular vibrating technique. Pressure can be moderate to very heavy.

Either in conjunction with or independent of the above, you may employ petrissage and/or the judo chop technique on the deltoids, lower trapezius, and teres major.

There are no specific erotic techniques for the neck and shoulders; however, the relaxation that results from conventional massage should make R more receptive to sexual arousal.

To increase this receptivity, try the following very gentle massage:

R lies on his back. M places the fingers of one hand on R's neck just below the chin and above the Adam's apple. Using the fingertip stroking technique and a feather-light touch, proceed downward to the chest. Repeat as often as desired.

For further variation, each path of fingertip stroking might extend lower and lower toward the genitals. The maneuver might then end in genital caressing. For still further variation, substitute fingernail stroking or the consecutive fingertip maneuver for fingertip stroking.

Back

There are almost as many different types of back rub and back massage as there are masseurs and masseuses. The following three programs are widely accepted and relatively easy to perform.

Each program is multistage. It is recommended that you perform the stages exactly as presented here. However, if this proves too strenuous or difficult either for M or for R, you may eliminate stages at your discretion.

Program Number One: *Conditioning Massage*

1. M places both hands on the small of R's back just above the buttocks and about two inches to each side of the spinal column. Using the circular vibrating technique—but with the heels of the hands rather than with the fingers—describe circles approximately six inches in diameter. Trace paths from the small of the back to the shoulder blades (see figures 21 and 22). Pressure is always moderate to very heavy and exerted upward. Continue until entire back is covered.

Repeat as desired. Generally three repetitions will suffice, though R may want more; the technique is relaxing as well as conditioning, and the pressure normally feels very good.

2. Place two fingers on the spinous process of the seventh cervical vertebra (see diagram). Generally this is the uppermost vertebra that you can detect. Using the circular vibrating technique, move down the spinal column from vertebra to vertebra until you've reached the coccyx.

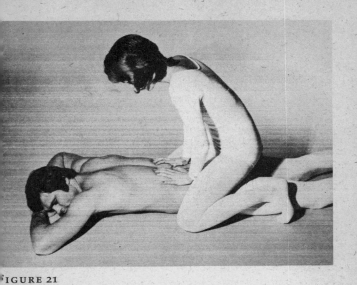

FIGURE 21

FIGURE 22

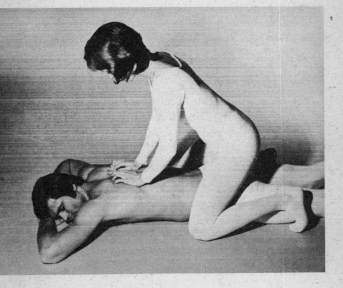

Continue to massage the area surrounding the coccyx with the circular vibrating technique, then retrace your route back up the spine to the seventh cervical vertebra.

Now go down the spine again, but this time apply pressure to the right side of each vertebra instead of directly atop it. When you reach the coccyx, work your way back up.

Repeat the above on the left side of the spine.

In all the above maneuvers pressure is moderately heavy and exerted toward the spine.

3. M places both hands on the small of R's back, as in Step 1. Repeat Step 1; however, this time, instead of applying pressure only with the heels of the hands, apply pressure with the entire hand—fingers, palms, heels. Diameter of circles should be six to nine inches. Pressure should be moderately heavy and exerted toward the heart.

4. Either in conjunction with or independent of the above, employ petrissage on the deltoids, lower trapezius, teres major, latissimus dorsi, and obliquus externus abdominis.

5. Either in conjunction with or independent of the above, employ the judo chop technique on the rib cage and thoracicolumbar fascia (posterior sheet). (See figure 7, p. 35.) Cupped-hand tapotement may be used instead of judo chop.

6. If Step 4 and/or 5 is employed, complete the conditioning back massage by repeating Step 3.

Program Number Two: *Relaxing Massage*

1. Place your hands on R's trapezius muscles with your thumbs resting directly over the spine (see

figure 7, p. 35). Using the circular vibrating technique, massage the area surrounding the spine with your thumbs. Pressure should be moderate to very heavy and should be exerted toward the spine.

Maneuver your thumbs as far up the neck and toward the hairline as they will reach while your hands are still in place on the outer surfaces of the trapezius muscles. Then, still keeping your hands in place, maneuver your thumbs as far down the spine as they will reach.

2. Place both hands on R's upper back about two inches away from the spine. Using the circular vibrating technique—but with the heels of the hands rather than with the fingers—describe circles approximately six inches in diameter. Trace paths from the shoulder blades to the small of the back, then return. Pressure should be moderately to very heavy and exerted downward. Continue until the entire back has been covered.

3. Repeat Step 2, using the middle three fingers of each hand instead of the heels of the hands. While fingers are performing the circular vibrating technique, thumbs are resting next to spine, supporting your weight on R's back. Pressure is moderately to very heavy and exerted downwards.

4. Place one palm on each of R's shoulders, and press down hard. Now, without releasing this pressure, begin performing the circular vibrating technique with the heels of your hands, thus applying even more pressure. Now release all pressure, rest several seconds, then repeat the exercise. Continue as desired. Generally three repetitions will suffice, though R may want more; the technique is extremely relaxing, and the pressure normally feels very good.

5. Place both hands on R's upper back about four inches away from the spine. Resting your weight on your palms, perform the circular vibrating technique with your thumbs, which should be about an inch away from the spine.

Trace down the sides of the spine to the coccyx (see figure 7, p. 35), then back up to the shoulder blades. Pressure should be moderately to very heavy and exerted toward the spine.

6. Either in conjunction with or independent of the above, employ petrissage on the deltoids, lower trapezius, teres major, latissimus dorsi, and obliquus externus abdominis (see figure 7, p. 35).

7. Either in conjunction with or independent of the above, employ the judo chop technique on R's rib cage and thoracicolumbar fascia (posterior sheet). (See figure 7, p. 35.)

8. Whether or not Step 6 and/or 7 is performed, complete the relaxing back massage with the following exercise:

Place both hands on the small of R's back just above the buttocks and about two inches to each side of the spine. Using the circular vibrating technique — but applying pressure with the entire hand rather than merely with the fingers — describe circles approximately six inches in diameter. Trace paths from the small of the back to the shoulder blades.

Pressure is always moderately to very heavy and extended upward. Continue until entire back is covered.

Program Number Three: *Erotic Massage*

Place both hands on R's trapezius muscles, between the shoulders and neck. Then slowly lift your

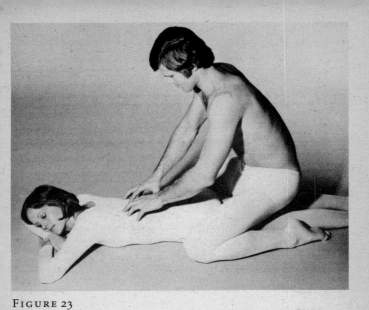

FIGURE 23

FIGURE 24

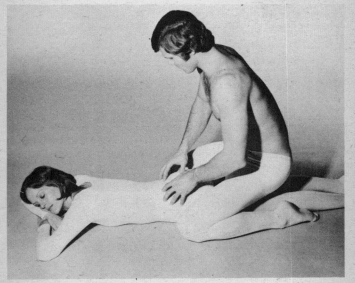

palms so that only your fingertips are touching R's flesh.

Draw the fingertips slowly over R's back, continuing downward to the buttocks (see figures 23 and 24). Use a feather-light touch, and repeat as often as desired.

For variation, each path of fingertip stroking might extend lower and lower. Stroke into the cleft between the buttocks, then to the perineum and genitals.

For further variation, substitute fingernail stroking or the consecutive fingertip maneuver for fingertip stroking.

Though uncomplicated, these techniques are quite effective.

Arms

Relaxing and conditioning techniques for massaging the arms are numerous. Those described in the following paragraphs are among the more effective and the easiest to administer.

Satisfactory massage of the arms does not require use of the full ensemble of techniques. Merely select the two or three that you find easiest to administer or that R finds most satisfying.

1. Clutch R's arm at the wrist between the thumb and index finger of both your hands. Now turn one of your hands in one direction and the other in the opposite direction; the effect is that the area near R's wrist is simultaneously rubbed with a clockwise movement by one of your hands and a counterclockwise movement by the other.

Continue up the forearm and upper arm to the shoulder, then back down. Repeat once or twice.

2. A variation on the above: Instead of gripping

R's arm between thumb and index finger, grip it with your entire hand. Use both hands, of course, and proceed exactly as above.

3. Perform petrissage on the biceps, triceps, flexor carpi, and extensor carpi radialis (see figure 6, p. 34).

4. Perform the judo chop technique on the biceps, triceps, flexor carpi, and extensor carpi radialis.

5. Put two fingers or your thumb on R's brachial vein just below the armpit. Using the circular vibrating technique, work your way down the arm, switching to the cephalic vein at the elbow. When you reach the wrist, retrace your route. Pressure is always exerted upward and is firm but not heavy.

6. Using two fingers and the circular vibrating technique, massage the entire arm from wrist to shoulder.

7. Using your thumb and the circular vibrating technique, massage the area around the elbow. Pressure should be heavy. Then with firm but light pressure perform the circular vibrating motion with two fingers in the elbow pit. Continue up the bicep to the armpit.

8. Using two fingers and the circular vibrating technique, massage the entire armpit and bordering areas of the rib cage, pectoral muscle, and latissimus dorsi. In conjunction with this exercise you might also perform petrissage on the bordering areas of the pectoral and latissimus dorsi muscles.

9. Take R's hand in yours. Using your thumb and the circular vibrating technique, massage the muscles of the palm and thumb. Next, massage the muscles below the finger joints. Then massage the muscles of the wrist.

Now take R's little finger, fleshy side up, on your

palm. Using the circular vibrating technique, massage each joint with your thumb. Then massage the cushion of the finger.

Now massage R's other fingers and thumb in the same manner. After you've massaged each finger individually, take all five of them between your palms, and move your hands in large, sweeping, circular motions.

Now turn R's hand over. With one of your hands grip R's hand at the wrist. With the thumb of your other hand massage the back of R's hand. Work from the wrist toward the fingers. Exert pressure toward the wrist. Massage around the joints of each finger and between the fingers. Perform circular vibrating motions on each finger, using your thumb. Then massage each joint. End by massaging the fingernails.

10. No matter which of the above techniques you employ and which you omit, end the arm massage by performing the circular vibrating technique with two fingers on the entire arm.

The above techniques are both relaxing and conditioning. There are no specific erotic techniques to be applied to the arms; however, the relaxation that results from conventional massage should make R more receptive to sexual arousal.

To increase that receptivity, try one of the following gentle massages:

1. Perform light fingertip stroking of R's entire arm, from shoulder to fingertips and back. You may favor either the outer or the inner surface, or divide your attentions between the two. Repeat as desired.

2. Substitute fingernail stroking or the consecutive

fingertip maneuver for fingertip stroking in the maneuver described above.

3. Using the consecutive fingertip technique and a feather-light touch, brush one specific area of the arm a number of times. The technique is most effective on the inner side of the forearm, inner side of the upper arm, or in the armpit. Your strokes should be downward toward the wrist.

Note: In many people the armpit is an extremely sensitive area sexually. Experiment with caressing it during sex play; the chances are good that these experiments will heighten your partner's arousal.

Legs and Buttocks

The lower legs and feet are generally rather insensitive to erotic stimulation. The thighs and buttocks are usually quite sensitive to such stimulation. Before examining specific arousal techniques designed to take advantage of this sensitivity, let us investigate relaxing and conditioning techniques.

As with the arms relaxing and conditioning techniques for massaging the legs are numerous. Those described in the following paragraphs are among the more effective and the easiest to administer.

Satisfactory massage of the legs does not require use of the full ensemble of techniques. Merely select the two or three that you find easiest or that R finds most satisfying.

1. R lies on his back. M applies two fingers to the inner side of one of R's legs just below the groin. Using the circular vibrating technique, massage

the entire groin area, following a horizontal path from buttock to hip. Exert pressure upward. Your touch should be firm and heavy; the purpose of this maneuver is to relax and condition, not to cause sexual arousal.

Next, locate the femoral vein just below the groin on the inside of the leg (see figure 25). Using two fingers and the circular vibrating technique, follow the vein down to the great saphenous vein, then follow the great saphenous vein to the ankle. Pressure should be firm and exerted upward.

2. Perform petrissage on the muscles of the thigh, calf, and buttocks.

FIGURE 25

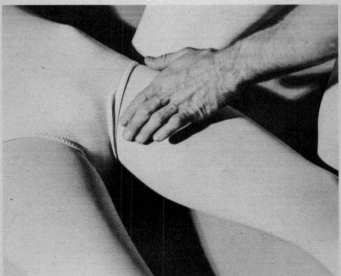

3. Perform the judo chop technique on the muscles of the thigh, calf, and buttocks.

4. Using four fingers and the circular vibrating technique, massage the entire leg from ankle to hip. Pressure should be moderately heavy and exerted upward.

5. Using your thumb and the circular vibrating technique, massage the area around the kneecap. Pressure should be heavy. Then with firm but light to moderate pressure perform the circular vibrating motion with three fingers in the knee pit. Continue up the great saphenous and femoral veins to the groin.

6. Using two fingers and the circular vibrating technique, massage the area surrounding the ankle-bone. Pressure should be moderately heavy and exerted upward. Next, massage the upper surface of the foot, from ankle to toe. Then, using your thumb and the circular vibrating technique, massage the sole of the foot from heel to toe.

Now, using your thumb and the circular vibrating technique, massage the bottom joint of the big toe. Pressure should be firm and exerted toward the foot. Next, using your thumb and index finger, perform the circular vibrating motion on the next joint of the toe. Then similarly massage the cushion of the toe and the toenail.

Repeat this procedure with the other toes.

7. No matter which of the above techniques you employ and which you omit, end the leg massage by performing the circular vibrating technique with four fingers on the entire leg.

Note: The same maneuvers in relaxing and conditioning massage should be performed on each leg. Equal attention should be devoted to the fronts and backs of the legs, with R alternately assuming prone and supine positions to permit easy access.

The relaxation that results from conventional massage of the legs should leave R in a frame of mind extremely conducive to sexual arousal. The following techniques should build upon the mood, creating intense sexual desire.

1. Using a feather-light stroke, run your fingertips from R's ankles to groin. Repeat, making the span shorter and shorter, starting now at the ankles, then midway toward the calf, then at the bottom of the calf, then midway up the calf, and so on, until you are stroking only the upper part of the thigh.

2. Same as above, except that you employ fingernail stroking instead of fingertip stroking.

3. Same as above, but substitute the consecutive fingertip maneuver.

4. Start just above the knee. Using a feather-light touch, stroke the thigh horizontally. With each stroke draw closer to the groin. Use either fingertips or fingernails.

5. Gently stroke the inside of the thigh with your palm. Pressure should be feather-light and exerted upward.

6. Letting your palm rest on the inside of the thigh, perform the consecutive fingertip maneuver close to R's groin.

7. Perform the consecutive fingertip maneuver in a stationary position high up on R's thigh. The position should be such that the fingertips are consecutively stroking the flesh of the thigh while the knuckles are brushing against R's genitals.

8. Using the tips of your fingers, trace a connected series of circles from knee to groin. Touch should be very light.

9. Same as above, but substitute fingernails for fingertips; again, use a very light touch.

10. Sitting behind R, grip the insides of both of R's thighs at the same time, reaching around from behind (and with your arms around R's waist). Bring your hands upward along the thighs until contact is made with R's genitals.

11. Same as above, except that instead of gripping the inside of R's thighs, you merely perform the consecutive fingertip maneuver along the insides of the thighs until you have reached the genitals.

12. In the same position as above perform the circular vibrating technique along the insides of both thighs. Use two fingers of each hand and a light touch.

13. Run your fingers up the outsides of R's thighs while your thumbs explore the insides and eventually R's groin.

14. Perform petrissage on the buttocks.

15. Clutching one buttock in each hand, move them vigorously in circular or lateral directions.

16. Gently and with a feather-light touch stroke the buttocks with your fingertips.

17. Same as above, but substitute fingernails for fingertips.

18. Perform the consecutive fingertip maneuver with one or both hands on R's buttocks; hand(s) should be positioned so that fingertips land in the cleft between the buttocks.

The above are a comparatively small number of arousal techniques that may be performed upon the legs and buttocks. The full range of possibilities is virtually infinite and is limited only by your imagination.

Attempt any combination of techniques that you think R might find interesting. You've nothing to lose and a great deal to gain.

A few points to keep in mind:

1. The insides and backs of the thighs are the most sensitive areas.

2. Part of the excitement in being touched in a sexual way comes from anticipation. Therefore, go about what you're doing very slowly, and don't always follow through as expected.

3. To heighten arousal, brush against the genitals, but refrain from direct genital stimulation until you've been given an indication that R is fully aroused.

4. With some women the buttocks are more sensitive than any organ other than the clitoris.

5. Part of the appeal of having one's buttocks stroked may be the anticipation of anal contact. You can heighten arousal by teasingly approaching then withdrawing from the anus. However, bear in mind that some people have an aversion to anal contact and may be turned off by this approach.

Chests and Breasts

For relaxing and conditioning massage of the chest employ one or more of the techniques listed below. When employing two or more techniques, employ them in the order in which they are presented here.

Because the female's breasts are protuberant and

sensitive, some techniques will have to be modified when R is a female. Never, when massaging a female, apply heavy pressure to the breasts.

The techniques:

1. Place three fingers of each hand on R's clavicle at the points where the clavicle meets the sternum (see figure 6, p. 34). Using the circular vibrating technique, work your way to the far ends of the clavicle. Pressure should be heavy and exerted downward.

Next, trace similar horizontal paths immediately below the clavicle. Continue in this manner until you have reached the lowermost point of the sternum. In each path proceed until your outward motion reaches the shoulders or (farther down the torso) the latissimus dorsi (see figure 6, p. 34). When R is female, massage only the upper portions of the breasts; these upper portions are muscular and contain none of the sensitive tissue of the lower portions.

Finally, perform the circular vibrating technique on those lower areas of the rib cage that have not yet been covered.

2. Perform petrissage on the pectoral muscles (see figure 6, p. 34). If R is female, avoid the protuberant portions of the breasts; confine your attentions to the upper, muscular portions.

3. If R is male, perform the judo chop technique over the entire rib cage. If R is female, perform the judo chop technique over every portion of the rib cage that can be struck without coming into contact with the protuberant portions of the breasts.

4. Place the heel of your hand over the lowermost portion of the sternum. Employ the circular vibrating technique with heavy pressure exerted upward.

Then cover the bottom outline of the rib cage, continuing to perform the circular vibrating technique with the heel of your hand.

5. Repeat Step 1, substituting the heel of the hand for the fingers.

The breasts may be sexually responsive in males as well as in females. Thus, while anatomical differences lessen the variety of breast-stimulation techniques that may be performed on males, the fact remains that stimulation of the male's breasts will often be a significant factor in evoking his optimal sexual response.

The following techniques of erotic massage may be performed on both males and females:

1. Place two fingers of one hand atop the upper portion of one of R's breasts, just below the clavicle. Using the circular vibrating technique and featherlight pressure, massage the entire breast, exerting pressure downward. Then massage the other breast similarly.

2. Pinch R's nipples gently between your thumb and index finger.

3. Run your fingers over R's breasts as if you were performing petrissage but without actually lifting the flesh. Do this to both breasts at the same time. Touch should be feather-light.

4. Roll R's nipples between thumb and index finger.

5. Rapidly stroke one nipple with the tip of one finger.

6. Gently stroke the area of one areola with one fingertip (the areola is the area of pigmented flesh surrounding the nipple).

7. Stroke the areola and nipples gently with your fingernails.

8. Stroke the entire breast gently with your fingernails.

9. Perform the consecutive fingertip maneuver on the nipple, areola, and/or general lower portion of the breast.

10. Circle the areola rapidly with one fingertip, using a feather-light touch.

11. Stroke the entire breast gently with your fingertips.

If R is female, the following additional maneuvers may be employed:

1. Cup one breast in each hand, and rotate them in circular patterns.

2. Using a feather-light touch, stroke the sides of the breasts with your fingertips.

3. Cupping one breast in each hand, push them gently but firmly upward toward R's face.

4. Cupping one breast in each hand, gently but firmly pinch the areolae and nipples.

Abdomen

For relaxing and conditioning massage of the abdomen perform one or more of the following exercises:

1. Using two or three fingers of one hand and employing the circular vibrating technique, vigorously massage the entire central abdominal region (see figure 26). Pressure should be as heavy as R can bear and should be exerted upward.

2. Using the heel of one hand, make large circles on the same region. Again, pressure should be as heavy as R can bear and should be exerted upward.

3. Perform petrissage on the entire abdomen—i.e., the region described above, plus the areas of the oblique muscles (see figure 6, p. 34).

4. Perform the judo chop technique on the central abdomen (region boxed in diagram). For maximum effectiveness R should lie on his back and lift his feet about three inches off the floor, thereby tensing the abdominal muscles. M then vigorously pounds the entire area with a rain of judo chops—the harder, the better. At the beginning of a program of massage start moderately and build up to more forceful blows.

FIGURE 26

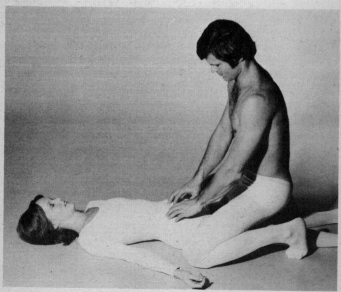

5. With the heel of each hand on one side of the torso perform the circular vibrating technique from armpit to hip. Pressure should be very heavy and exerted upward.

6. Using three fingers of one hand and the circular vibrating technique, trace a circle around the navel. Pressure should be as hard as R can bear and exerted upward.

7. Using three fingers of one hand and the circular vibrating technique, cover the entire region from the waist to the groin. Pressure should be moderately to very heavy and exerted upward.

For erotic effect employ feather-light fingertip or fingernail stroking in any of the above maneuvers. Additional erotic techniques of abdomen massage are as follows:

1. Place one fingertip in R's navel, and gently describe small circles.

2. Using fingertip stroking and a feather-light touch, describe a straight line from the navel to the genitals. One to four fingers may be employed.

3. Same as 2, but use fingernails instead of fingertips.

4. Same as 2, but perform the consecutive fingertip maneuver from navel to genitals.

5. Using fingertips, slowly and gently stroke the entire abdomen. (Don't underestimate the value of this simple maneuver. The abdomen is extremely sensitive, and intense sexual arousal can be brought about merely through uncomplicated stroking of this sort.)

6. Same as 5, but use palm instead of fingertips.

7. Same as 5, but use fingernails instead of fingertips.

8. Touch one index finger to each side of R's lower abdomen just above the pelvis and atop the outer termini of the inguinal ligament (see figure 6, p. 34). Using a feather-light touch and the circular vibrating technique, trace a path along the inguinal ligament to the genitals.

9. Place both thumbs on R's navel, and let your fingertips fall naturally into place on both sides. Now, very slowly, move your thumbs downward to the genitals while performing the consecutive fingertip maneuver with your descending fingertips.

Note: With the exception of No. 9, all the above erotic maneuvers can be performed with one hand while the other hand performs other erotic maneuvers on other parts of the body.

Ano-Perineal Region

The anus is the terminal end of the rectum, the opening through which solid wastes pass from the body. The perineum is the fleshy triangular area that separates the anus and the genitals.

Both areas are rich in erogenous nerve endings. Properly stimulated, they can cause intense sexual arousal.

Remember, however, that most women and many men are not responsive to direct stimulation of extremely sensitive areas unless the stage has first been set with kissing, caressing, and other foreplay involving less sensitive areas. Before attempting ano-perineal stimulation, be sure your partner is ready for it.

Also remember that some people have an aversion to anal contact. If your partner indicates that he or she has such an aversion, you should not attempt such stimulation.

The following techniques are recommended for stimulation of the ano-perineal region:

1. Using one or two fingers and the circular vibrating technique, massage the entire perineum. Pressure should be light to moderate and should be exerted toward the genitals. Your fingers may touch the genitals or the anus, but prolonged contact with these organs should not take place.

2. Same as above, except that instead of applying light to moderate pressure, you simply let your fingertips graze gently over the region.

3. Same as above, but use fingernails instead of fingertips. Be *very* gentle.

4. Gently run one or two fingers through the hair of the perineum and anus. The fingers should not actually touch the flesh. (This can be extremely arousing.)

5. Place two fingers on the perineum about an inch apart. Applying firm pressure, vibrate the fingers in place.

6. On the male place the index finger on one side and the middle finger on the other side of the base of the penis (from beneath — i.e., on perineal side of — the testicles). Applying moderately heavy pressure, run fingers back and forth along penile column but without lifting them (thus, they move back and forth along an area less than one inch long).

7. On the male perform the circular vibrating technique around the base of the penis. Pressure should be moderate and exerted toward the penis.

8. On the male perform the circular vibrating technique *on*—rather than around—the base of the penis. Pressure should be moderate and exerted toward the center of the penile column.

9. Place one finger over R's anus, covering the aperture completely. Perform the circular vibrating technique. Pressure should be moderate to heavy.

10. Place the upper surface of one hand—i.e., the semicircular surface comprising the inner side of the thumb and the outer side of the index finger—inside the cleft between the buttocks. The knuckle of the index finger should be over the anus. With this knuckle perform the circular vibrating technique. Pressure should be moderate and directed upward.

11. Same as above with an additional element: While performing the circular vibrating technique with your knuckle, stroke R's perineum with any fingers that reach it and stroke the upper reaches of the cleft between the buttocks with your thumb.

12. Place the tips of four fingers in the cleft between R's buttocks. They should make only light contact with the flesh. The middle finger should be even with the anus. Now, without moving the rest of your hand, perform the consecutive fingertip maneuver.

13. Lifting your fingers slightly from the position described above, perform the consecutive fingertip maneuver, touching only the hairs of the anus and those in the cleft between the buttocks.

14. With a feather-light touch perform the consecutive fingertip maneuver against the perineum.

15. Perform the consecutive fingertip maneuver touching only the hairs of the perineum, not the flesh.

Male Genitals

There is almost no wrong way to touch the male genitals.

Facetiousness aside, the genitals are extremely sensitive erogenously; any way of touching them, provided that pain is not inflicted, will arouse the average man.

The following techniques, properly executed, are particularly stimulating:

1. Start at R's knee. Using fingertips or fingernails, stroke very lightly up the thigh to the groin, across the scrotum, and down the opposite thigh to the knee. Repeat in the opposite direction, this time letting the final stroke stop somewhat short of the knee.

Continue in this manner, making each stroke progressively shorter until your strokes are limited to within a few inches of the genitals. Then grip the scrotum in one hand, and knead it very gently.

2. Gently grip the flesh beneath the glans; with two fingers of the opposite hand perform the circular vibrating technique on the glans. Pressure should be extremely light.

3. Hold the penis at the glans so that the underside of the stem is exposed. Using two fingers, gently perform the circular vibrating technique up and down the stem.

4. Same as above, but instead of performing the circular vibrating technique, simply stroke the underside of the penis with your fingertips.

5. Same as above, except use fingernails—*very* gently—in place of fingertips.

6. Take the glans in your palm. Perform the con-

secutive fingertip maneuver on the underside of the penis while your thumb rests on the upper surface.

7. Take the penile stem in your palm. Perform the consecutive fingertip maneuver. (Exercises 6 and 7 are two of the most arousing you can perform.)

8. Gently grip the flesh beneath the glans. With the palm of your opposite hand very gently massage the glans.

9. Gently grip the penis at the glans, holding the glans so that the penis is roughly parallel to the ground. Stroke the upper surface of the penis with your fingernails or fingertips.

10. Take one testicle in each hand, and knead gently.

11. Slowly trace circles around the corona of the penis with your thumb or fingertip.

12. Holding the penis by the glans, use your opposite hand to gently stroke the scrotum. Employ either fingertips or fingernails.

13. Using two fingers, perform the circular vibrating technique on the area covered by pubic hair. Pressure should be moderate and directed toward the penis.

14. Gripping the testicles gently with one hand, slowly stroke the glans with the fingertips of the other.

15. Same as above, using fingernails in place of fingertips.

All the above maneuvers can be performed whether the penis is flaccid or erect. Most, of course, will produce erection in a very short time.

The following maneuvers can be performed successfully only upon an erect penis:

1. Holding the penis firmly at the glans, use two

fingers of your opposite hand to perform the circular vibrating technique on the penile stem. Pressure should be moderate and should cover every surface of the stem.

2. Gently but firmly grip the penis in one hand, and move the hand slowly up and down the entire length of the stem.

3. Gripping the penis as above, describe circles with your opposite palm on the surface of the glans. This action may be performed simultaneously with the up-and-down motion described in Exercise 2.

4. Same as above, except the palm maneuver is replaced by slowly tracing circles around the corona with your thumb or fingertip.

5. With your thumb and index finger squeeze the sides of the penis as vigorously as you can. Move up and down penile stem as you squeeze.

6. With one hand perform the maneuver described in Exercise 2. With the opposite hand gently massage the testicles, using very light petrissage.

7. Rub the glans very vigorously back and forth across R's abdomen.

8. Gripping the penis at its base, move it from one side to the other as far as it will go.

9. Grip the penis scissorslike at its base, using your index and middle fingers. The penis should rest at the juncture of the two fingers, and the fingers themselves should extend downward behind the testicles. To accomplish this, your hand must be over the penis and with your palm facing downward. In this position your palm will be touching the upper surface of the penile stem.

Now with your thumb and little finger encircle the penile stem. Knead the testicles with your middle and index fingers while performing an up-and-down motion with your palm, thumb, and little finger.

Almost needless to say, many of the above maneuvers can be performed in combination with others. Your only limits in experimenting with these techniques should be the limits of your imagination and your partner's desires.

Female Genitals

The female genitals, particularly the clitoris, are as sensitive as the male genitals. However, most women are incapable of responding to immediate genital stimulation. The stage must first be set with kissing, caressing, and other foreplay.

Before attempting any of the following techniques, be sure that your partner is sufficiently aroused.

1. Using one or two fingers, gently perform the circular vibrating technique on the flesh that is covered by pubic hair.

2. Gently run your fingertips over the area covered by pubic hair.

3. Gently run your fingertips *through* the pubic hair without touching the flesh.

4. Using the bottommost knuckle of the index finger, gently massage the pubic bone just above the clitoris.

5. Take the clitoris between the tips of your index and middle fingers. Gently but briskly run the fingers along its sides.

6. Run one finger gently but briskly across the clitoris.

7. Same as above, except that your motion is up and down the long axis of the clitoris instead of across its short axis.

8. Perform the consecutive fingertip maneuver on the clitoris.

9. Place your index and middle fingers between the labia majora. Gently but quickly move the fingers back and forth.

10. Insert the fingers deeper, so that they are between the labia minora. Perform the same back-and-forth motion.

11. Take one of the labia minora between thumb and index finger, and gently rub it.

12. Insert one or two fingers into the vagina and gently rub the vaginal walls.

13. Same as above, except that you fondle the cervix.

14. Same as above, but explore the cul-de-sac behind and surrounding the cervix.

15. Same as above, except that you rotate your fingers back and forth like the agitator of a washing machine.

16. With two fingers in the vagina move the fingers alternately back and forth.

17. With one or more fingers in the vagina massage the clitoris with your thumb.

18. Same as above, except that you trace circles around the base of the clitoris with your thumb.

19. Insert your thumb into the vagina, and massage the vaginal walls. At the same time stroke the thighs or perineum with your other four fingers.

20. Same as above, but knead the buttocks with your four fingers.

Oral Massage

There is almost no part of the body that will not respond to oral stimulation. Among the areas that are particularly responsive, in addition to the breasts, the genitals, and the ano-perineal region, are:

1. The ears.
2. The throat.
3. The armpits and the insides of the arms.
4. The abdomen.
5. The thighs, particularly on the insides and rear.

Although the effects of the tongue are very different from those of manual stimulation, oral stimulation creates highly pleasurable sensations in most recipients.

7

*Massage with
Vibrators and Other
Appliances*

Not surprisingly, technology, which has made its influence felt in so many areas of our lives, is making its influence felt in the world of massage also.

Today's masseur and masseuse have available many machines and devices that can broaden the range of sensations experienced during a massage.

The following are some of the more popular:

Vibrators

Vibrators can be used both in relaxing and conditioning massage and in erotic massage. They come in a variety of shapes, sizes, and price ranges.

Battery-Operated Vibrator

The battery-operated vibrator is a simple plastic-covered phallic-shaped device available at most department stores, pharmacies, and sundry shops. The price is usually under three dollars.

The advertisements and publicity materials for these vibrators stress that they can be used to massage the face, neck, feet, et cetera. They can, of course, but they're virtually worthless for that purpose. Their intended use—manufacturers' claims to the contrary notwithstanding—is to stimulate the sexual organs, particularly the female genitals.

They do a rather good job of it. The sensations created by contact with a vibrator are usually considerably more intense than sensations resulting from routine genital stimulation, and many couples find that their sex lives improve substantially as a result.

Until fairly recently, sexologists at best were skeptical about vibrators and at worst condemned them across the board. Now most sexologists recommend them, especially for women who complain that they are unable to get aroused or who, if arousable, are unable to have orgasm.

Dr. William H. Masters and Mrs. Virginia E. Johnson, celebrated for their widely circulated studies *Human Sexual Response* and *Human Sexual Inadequacy*, found that women who had previously been unable to achieve orgasm were able to do so with the aid of a vibrator.

The women simply applied the vibrator to the clitoris or to the area surrounding it. This stimulation resulted in orgasm. After several successful orgasms with the vibrator many of the women developed the ability to have orgasm during conventional sex relations.

Women may apply the vibrator themselves, or a man may apply it. Likewise, a woman may apply the vibrator to a man's genitals, or he may apply it himself.

In the Masters-Johnson experiments men who had difficulty getting or sustaining erection were helped by using a vibrator. Some men who were previously partially or totally impotent developed the ability to have full and lasting erections after a few sessions in which a female partner applied a vibrator to the penis, testicles, and ano-perineal region.

The battery-powered vibrator may be used to stimulate the female genitals in the following ways:

1. Lightly touch the tip or side of the vibrator to the clitoris.

2. Gently run the tip of the vibrator up and down one or both sides of the clitoral shaft.

3. Lightly press the side of the vibrator against the vulva and perineum.

4. Gently probe the vulva and ano-perineal region with the tip of the vibrator.

5. Insert the vibrator into the vagina. Apply light pressure with the side of the vibrator toward the clitoris.

The battery-powered vibrator may be used to stimulate the male genitals in the following ways:

1. Lightly touch the tip or side of the vibrator to the glans or the penile shaft.

2. Gently run the tip of the vibrator around the corona.

3. Gently probe the testicles and the ano-perineal region with the tip of the vibrator.

4. Hold the testicles in one hand. With the other roll the side of the vibrator over the entire exposed surface of the scrotum.

5. Roll the side of the vibrator over the penile stem.

6. Place the penis flat across your hand, which is held palm up. Now grip both penis and vibrator firmly in your fingers, and turn the vibrator on.

Pistol-Grip Electric Vibrator

The pistol-grip electric vibrator is a sturdy machine designed for barbers, chiropractors, and professional masseurs and masseuses. Some are single-head units; others come with an assortment of inter-changeable heads — one for scalp massage, another for facial massage, another for body massage, et cetera. Prices range from five to thirty-five dollars.

For relaxing and conditioning massage merely apply the appropriate vibrator head to the part of the body you wish to massage. Move the head along the routes described in previous chapters on manual massage. Pressure may range from light to moder-ately heavy.

With the aid of an electric vibrator you will often be able to achieve muscular relaxation in a fraction of the time possible when massaging manually.

For erotic massage a smooth vibrator head is ap-plied gently to the genital organs and is moved over the organs slowly. Because the electric vibrator vi-brates with much more force and speed than the battery-powered vibrator, the former can provide a far more intense experience, though it has obvious limitations of shape and accessibility to the internal female genital structures.

Over-the-Hand Electric Vibrator

Like the pistol-grip vibrator, the over-the-hand vibrator is a professional machine. It consists of a vibrating unit which is attached with straps to the back of your hand, causing your fingers to vibrate. You then touch any part of the body with your fingers, just as you would in conventional massage. The cost is ten to thirty dollars.

As with the pistol-grip vibrator muscular relaxation can often be achieved in just a fraction of the time possible when massaging manually.

The over-the-hand vibrator is particularly good for facial massage.

For erotic massage simply touch the genital areas as you would normally, being careful, of course, not to bump the vibrating unit itself against sensitive areas of the body.

Whirlpools

Large professional whirlpool units have long been a favorite of physicians, trainers of athletic teams, and others who regularly treat sprains and other muscular ailments.

The injured muscles are immersed in hot, rapidly swirling water, which both relaxes and eases pain. Afterward, conventional massage techniques are employed to reinforce the whirlpool's effects.

Home whirlpool units have not, at this writing, appeared on the market. However, several units are available that permit you to convert a normal bathtub to whirlpool use. They range in price from fifty to two hundred dollars and can be purchased at bathroom specialty shops or large department stores.

Simply attach the unit to your bathtub, plug it in, and let the swirling water relax you. If tub size permits, you can share a whirlpool bath with a partner.

Though the whirlpool is primarily employed for relaxing, it can also be put to direct erotic use. Sit with your genitals directly in the stream of water and as close to the outlet as comfortably possible. The force of the water should prove arousing; some women report orgasm from this water pressure.

Shower Spray

Similar in erotic effect to the whirlpool is a steady stream of water produced from an ordinary shower head.

Simply stand with your genitals directly in the path of the spray, which should be needle-sharp and very forceful. Warm to moderately hot water is best; cold or too-hot water will destroy the erotic effect.

Not everyone will be turned on by this technique. Most men will be unable to respond to it, and a few women will be likewise indifferent. But most women will achieve at least some sexual arousal as the spray is trained upon the clitoris and other genital organs, and some women will be capable of achieving orgasm in this manner.

Somewhat more convenient than the American-style shower head is the hand-held shower unit commonly found in Europe. This unit permits you to train the spray very precisely on a given area of the body and to take advantage of the greater force that results from being closer to the spray.

Electric Toothbrush

One of the most effective devices for arousing a woman is a cordless electric or battery-powered toothbrush.

As with the battery-powered vibrator the side of the toothbrush cylinder may be applied to the external genitals, or the base may be inserted into the vagina.

For an especially intense erotic effect insert the

base of one electric toothbrush into the vagina; then, with the back of the brush from another unit—repeat, the *back* of the brush, *not* the bristles—lightly touch the clitoris.

The toothbrush cylinder may also, of course, be applied to the male genitals for erotic effect.

A Few Devices to Keep Away From

Whereas the above mechanical devices can be helpful in sexual stimulation, others that are presently on the market have been found useless or even harmful.

Stay away from:

The French tickler. This is a rubber condom with a number of small studs on its tip and along its sides. In theory these studs are supposed to stimulate the vagina in a way that the naked penis cannot.

It sounds good in theory, but it doesn't work. The vagina is almost totally insensitive. The female's sexual sensation comes principally from stimulation of the clitoris, which the French tickler does not touch.

The coronal ring. This is a circular device which fits around the top of the penis just below the glans. It is made up of one or two rings of spherical rubber or plastic studs.

In theory it works just like the French tickler. And in practice, like the French tickler, it doesn't work at all.

The clitoral brush. This is a toothbrushlike device which protrudes from a ring placed around the base of the penis just before coitus. The brush is supposed to stimulate the clitoris while normal coital movements are taking place.

Again, the theory is fine. But the brush does not consistently come into contact with the clitoris. When it does, it tends to irritate rather than satisfy. And if the man leans a bit too hard, the clitoris may be badly bruised.

8

---

*Massage with Creams
and Lotions*

CREAMS and lotions can enhance the effects of both relaxing and conditioning massage and erotic massage.

Creams and lotions applied before or during massage will keep the skin from chafing. Rubbed on after massage, they serve as a luxurious and fragrant final touch.

They can also be used to heighten the sensations of erotic massage.

To keep the skin from chafing, use a lotion or cream with a moisturizing ingredient and no astringent or alcoholic content. Take a small amount on your fingertips, and apply it to R's skin via the circular vibrating technique. The smoothness of the lotion or cream against R's flesh will enhance the relaxing effect of your massage.

In addition to being mild and moisturizing, the lotion or cream used at the end of massage should exude a light and attractive scent. The cool moisture will feel especially pleasant after your rubdown, and the sweet fragrance will provide an extra fillip to an already delightful sensual experience.

Some professionals end a massage with an alcohol rub. Critics of the practice claim that its only effect is to separate the customer from a few extra dollars, because the alcohol does nothing to or for the body.

Actually, however, an alcohol rub can accomplish several purposes. First, it closes the pores, which is an important consideration if R is going outside into a temperature ten degrees colder than that of the massage room or if, no matter what the temperature, R is going to be exposed to dust, grime, et cetera. Second, alcohol dries quickly on the skin and serves as a bracer. Finally, its fragrance is pleasant and refreshing.

Of course, if you end a massage with an alcohol rub, do not also apply a cream or lotion.

To transform an ordinary back rub into an erotic one, place a bottle of mild, sweet-smelling lotion in your refrigerator about an hour before you begin.

Pour the refrigerated lotion directly onto R's back. The initial effect will be slightly shocking—and chilling. But as you rub the lotion deeply into R's flesh, he or she will begin to warm up all over.

Start at the shoulders, and work downward. By the time you reach the buttocks, R will be several degrees warmer.

You'll have a relaxed, grateful, and very eager lover on—as well as under—your hands.

To add special zing to erotic massage, pour some ordinary baby oil into your palms. Rub R's entire body with it, saving the genitals for last. Simultaneously, R should be applying oil to your body.

After genital massage, you're ready for coitus with both partners' bodies slick with oil. The effect is sensational.

9

Self-Massage

Most of us are familiar with tension and its effects: a tightening of the muscles, general irritability, narrowing of the attention span, troubled sleep, and a resultant loss of energy.

One of the best ways to relieve tension is through massage. If you don't have someone to massage you, perform the following ten-minute self-massage:

Whole-Body Relaxing Massage

1. Place the fingertips and thumb of one hand on the opposite wrist. Using the circular vibrating technique, work your way up the arm to the shoulder. Massage at three-inch intervals. Pressure should be light to moderate and should be exerted upward.

2. Perform petrissage on all the muscles of the same arm.

3. Place your opposite thumb in the elbow pit of the arm being massaged. Press down firmly. Now, with your index and middle fingers reach beneath the elbow. Place one of these fingers on each side of the elbow bone. Using the circular vibrating technique, vigorously massage the area surrounding the bone.

4. Take the hand of the arm being massaged between the thumb and index and middle fingers of the opposite hand. Using moderate to heavy pressure,

knead the entire hand—fingers, palm, back, wrist. Be especially attentive to the joints of the fingers and to the muscles of the palm.

5.
6. } Perform the same exercises
7. } on the opposite arm.
8.

9. Perform petrissage on the sternocleidomastoid and trapezius muscles (of the neck). (See figure 6, p. 34.)

10. Using the circular vibrating technique and moderate to heavy pressure, massage all accessible portions of the neck. Of course, when massaging the area over the windpipe, reduce pressure considerably. In all cases exert pressure downward.

11. Place the index and middle fingers of each hand on your opposite shoulder. Using the circular vibrating technique, vigorously cover the entire chest and abdominal area. Circles should be three inches in diameter; pressure should be heavy and exerted toward the center of the chest.

12. Perform petrissage on the pectoral muscles (see figure 6, p. 34).

13. Reaching cross-armed with each hand under the opposite armpit, perform petrissage on all accessible areas of the latissimus dorsi muscles (see figure 7, p. 35).

14. Place the fingertips and thumb of one hand on one ankle. Using the circular vibrating technique, work your way up and around the leg to the groin. Massage at three-inch intervals. Pressure should be moderate to heavy and should be exerted upward.

15. Perform petrissage on all muscles of the same leg.

16. Place both thumbs in the knee pit. Press firmly. With fingers perform the circular vibrating technique on the area surrounding the knee bone. Pressure should be very heavy and exerted upward.

17. Take the foot between the thumbs and fingers of both hands. Using heavy pressure, knead the entire foot. Be especially attentive to the joints of the toes and to the area surrounding the ankle.

18.
19. } Perform the same exercises
20. } on the opposite leg.
21.

22. Perform petrissage on both buttocks.

23. Place your thumbs in the small of your back as close as possible to the lowermost point of the spine. Using the circular vibrating technique and very heavy pressure, work your way as far upward as possible. Now return the thumbs to the lower portion of the back but slightly farther apart. Continue to work parallel paths up the back until all accessible areas have been covered.

24. Using the index and middle fingers of both hands, perform the circular vibrating technique on the groin. Massage across each inguinal ligament (see figure 6, p. 34), down to the perineum. Pressure should be moderate to heavy and should be exerted upward.

The above regimen, performed briskly, should take no longer than ten minutes.

Use it immediately upon waking to put you in a pleasant and relaxed mood for the day ahead. Or use it in the evening after a tense and difficult day; you'll feel almost as good as if you'd just taken a two-hour nap.

Or massage yourself to sleep at night: you'll probably relax more and sleep more peacefully than you have for ages.

The regimen may be performed in whole or in part. If performed in part, still observe the sequence of body parts as they are listed.

The regimen is particularly effective when combined with a program of calisthenics: ideally twenty push-ups, ten cross-toe touches, fifty sit-ups, ten leg rises, and twenty jumping jacks.

Facial Conditioning Massage

Perform the following facial self-massage each night before retiring. Within three to four weeks your facial muscles should take on a new and young-looking tautness, your cheeks should begin to flush with natural color, and your skin should start to glow.

This regimen is a favorite of models and actresses and is widely practiced by professional masseurs and masseuses throughout Europe.

1. Place the index and middle fingers of each hand directly below the corresponding earlobe. Using the circular vibrating technique at half-inch intervals, massage your neck along your jawline until your hands meet. Continue to trace parallel horizontal paths until you have covered the entire front side of the neck. Pressure should be moderate to heavy and should be exerted downward.

2. Place the index and middle fingers of each hand alongside the corresponding corners of your mouth. Using the circular vibrating technique at half-inch

intervals, work your way up and over your cheek-bones to the hairline. Continue to trace parallel paths until you have covered the entire face. Pressure should be moderate and should be exerted downward.

3. Place one finger on each side of your nose. Applying moderate pressure, slowly trace the line of your cheekbone as it goes under your eye and up to your temple. Repeat five times.

4. Using the circular vibrating technique and the index and middle fingers, massage the forehead, nose, and chin. Pressure should be moderate to heavy and should be exerted downward.

5. Close your eyes. Place the middle and index fingers of each hand on the corresponding eyelid. Very lightly perform the circular vibrating technique over the entire eye.

6. Complete your massage by performing very light petrissage on the muscles of the face.

10

Japanese Massage

AMONG the oldest practitioners of the arts of massage are the Japanese. Their techniques range from the extremely tender to the extremely vigorous. Some techniques are employed exclusively for pleasurable ends, others solely for therapeutic purposes; the majority serve multiple goals.

The most sensual of Japan's institutions of massage is the bath—an institution Westerners normally identify with the ancient Romans. Actually, the bath was developed independently in the Orient and has been refined considerably in recent centuries by the Japanese.

In Japan, as in ancient Rome, the bath does not serve a merely hygienic function. It also relaxes, conditions, provides sensual pleasure, and plays a social role.

It is not uncommon for an entire Japanese family to bathe together in a public bath. Nor is it uncommon for a tired Japanese businessman to rejuvenate his spirits with a long, relaxing bath in either a public bathing place or the privacy of his own bathroom.

In the Japanese home, by the way, the bathroom is separate and apart from the toilet facilities. The entire room is, in effect, a bath, with a drain in the center of the floor or on the side along a wall. The tub is circular and often large enough to accommodate two squatting people.

Since it is unthinkable for a Japanese to get into a tub while he is dirty, the actual cleaning of the body takes place outside the tub. The bather stands next to the tub. Using water scooped up from the tub, he douses himself thoroughly. He then soaps himself and rinses off with more water scooped from the tub. Only when he deems himself fully clean does he squat in the tub and relax.

In public baths, which are rather like miniature swimming pools, benches are built into the sides. Bathers sit and read or chat while bathing. As in the home, bathers clean themselves before entering the tub.

The chances are very good that you don't have facilities in your home to duplicate the Japanese bath exactly. However, with improvisation and a little imagination you should be able to adapt the techniques of the Japanese to your own circumstances.

The following program incorporates the most popular Japanese techniques. Naturally you don't have to perform all steps to enjoy it; but you will probably find that the more closely you stick to the format, the better your partner will like it.

1. M and R get into the shower together. Make the water as hot as you can stand it. Douse yourselves thoroughly. Then lower the temperature of the water, and stay under the spray for about two minutes.

During this time gently embrace and caress each other.

2. Step back from under the shower head. Now M takes a bar of soap and vigorously massages R with it.

Start by standing behind R and applying the soap to his or her shoulders and back. Then kneel and attend to the buttocks and the backs of the legs. Don't neglect the crevice between the buttocks.

Next, R turns around, and M attends to the front of the body — first the neck, chest, and arms, then, kneeling, the abdomen, legs, and genitals. Don't neglect the underarms.

Remember to apply the bar of soap itself to the skin, not merely your own soaped hands. And do it vigorously. The purpose of this step of the treatment is not to tease R into sexual arousal but to wake up R's body so that it will be responsive to future arousal maneuvers.

Of course, don't be vigorous to the point of inflicting pain. If R says it hurts, ease up a bit.

3. When R has been thoroughly soaped, go over the same bodily areas with your hands, working the soap into a lather.

Again, be vigorous. This is a toning, conditioning, and waking maneuver, not one aimed at sexual arousal.

4. R steps under the shower again. Using a washcloth or *tawashi* (a Japanese washcloth made of seaweed), scrub away the lather as vigorously as you can without inflicting pain.

The rough texture of the washcloth or *tawashi* will bring a healthy, ruddy glow to R's skin and wake up the body for the gentle, erotic maneuvers that will be performed later.

5. When R has been thoroughly scrubbed, step back from under the shower head. Now lather R again, but this time with soaped hands instead of directly with the bar of soap.

No need for vigorous rubbing this time. The purpose of this maneuver is to relax and soothe the body. Be gentle, using touch techniques described in Chapter 5.

6. When R is fully lathered again, perform a whole-body erotic massage.

First, stand directly in front of R. Now embrace R—your abdomen against R's, your arms either over or under R's. While in this position you will massage R's shoulders, back, and buttocks. Your touch should be gentle, soothing, arousing. You can add to your and R's enjoyment by kissing while massaging.

When you've ministered to all parts of the body that can be reached in this position—but not the genitals (save that for last)—kneel in front of R, and massage his or her legs. Work from thigh to ankle and back up, caressing both the front and the back of the legs.

Next, stand again, and move around behind R. Embracing from behind, massage R's neck, chest, and abdomen.

Finally, kneel again in front of R, and massage the genitals. If R is male, take one testicle in each hand, and knead gingerly. Massage the penis, the perineum, and the cleft between the buttocks. Rub lather into these organs while caressing them.

If R is female, gently lather the vulva, the perineum and the cleft between the buttocks. Do this slowly and thoroughly, using any of the techniques described in Chapter 6 that seem appropriate.

7. In the tub M sits behind R with legs around R's waist. Rub R's back for several minutes, using techniques described in Chapter 5. Then, reaching around R, massage chest, abdomen, legs, and genitals.

8. M sits in front of R with legs around R's waist

and massages R's chest, shoulders, arms, abdomen, and genitals.

9. M and R get out of the tub. Using a large terry-cloth towel, M dries R's entire body.

Supplementary Notes: The above program calls for one person to do all the massaging and the other to do all the enjoying. Sometimes this arrangement will be preferable, for it gives R a completely gratuitous treat, which can be employed as a sort of sexual gift or to create arousal under stressful circumstances. More often, however, a couple will desire mutual stimulation and satisfaction; in this case M and R switch roles at each step of the program.

The effects of a Japanese bath can be enhanced with lotions and creams, perfumes, et cetera. A nice touch is a bubble bath. Or if R is particularly weary or suffers muscular soreness after vigorous physical activity, a hot bath in salt water (one-half cup of salt in a full tub of water) should prove relaxing.

11

Swedish Massage

Swedish massage may be performed for therapeutic purposes but is more commonly employed for relaxing and conditioning.

Ideally, after a whole-body Swedish massage, R should be so relaxed that he or she is on the verge of sleep.

A full-scale, whole-body Swedish massage should last an hour. Most professional masseurs and masseuses in American health clubs, spas, et cetera can give one.

Swedish massage is taught in the United States at the Swedish Institute School for Massage and Allied Subjects, 154 West 71 Street, New York, N.Y. 10024.

Most of the massage techniques described in this book originate with the Swedes. Tapotement (the judo chop technique) and petrissage are two of the four basic techniques in the repertoire of every Swedish masseur or masseuse. The other two are effleurage and vibration.

Effleurage

With three or four fingers or with the entire flat of your hand, make whisk-broom strokes against R's flesh. Pressure should be moderate to heavy, and the stroke should be six to twelve inches long.

When stroking, always proceed in the direction of the heart. Thus, when stroking the legs, exert pressure upward; when stroking the neck, pressure is downward.

Vibration

Place one or more fingers against R's flesh. Press down firmly but gently. Now very quickly move the fingers back and forth on an axis.

This movement may be substituted for the circular vibrating technique in any of the exercises described in earlier chapters.

Sauna and Steam Baths

Swedish massage is particularly effective when performed after a sauna or steam bath. Most athletic clubs, health clubs, and large gynasiums have facilities for one or both.

If you don't have access to a bona fide sauna or steam bath, you can convert your own bathroom into a fairly accurate replica.

1. Close the windows and doors, and stuff all large cracks through which vapor might escape—for example, the crack at the bottom of the door, which can handily be stuffed with a towel.

2. Turn on the hot water in the shower. The tub should be plugged so that the water will not run out. The hotter the water, the better. When the tub is nearly full, pull the plug so that the water will not overflow. Then, as water level approaches zero, insert the plug again.

3. The average-size bathroom should become thick with water vapor within five to ten minutes.

4. Sit in the room for as long as you like, turning on the water for further vapor if needed.

Massage may be performed in the bathroom while the steam bath is being enjoyed or afterward. Here is a pleasant and stimulating program:

1. Take a steam bath. End it with a

2. hot shower. After lathering and rinsing yourself, slowly lower the temperature until you are taking an

3. ice-cold shower. Then

4. rub yourself dry, very vigorously, with a Turkish towel. Follow this with a

5. whole-body massage, then a refreshing

6. alcohol rub.

Naturally, this regimen is most enjoyable when performed upon you by someone else. But you can also perform it upon yourself if a partner is not available.

Massage with Willow Branches

In Sweden a sauna bath is often enhanced by a treatment with willow branches.

These may be used inside the sauna or afterward during relaxing and conditioning massage.

M gently strikes R's back with the branches for two to five minutes. The sensations created by this "whipping" are not painful but caressive, like the touch of a lover's lips on the skin.

Afterward, the back may be rubbed with creams, lotions, alcohol, et cetera.

Massage with Palm Leaves

Similar in action and effect to the willow-branch treatment is one with palm leaves. This Swedish massage technique can be combined with the previously described Japanese bath technique for a unique East-meets-West massage.

1. M and R get into the shower together. Make the water as hot as you can stand it. Douse yourselves thoroughly, then lower the temperature, and stay under the spray for two minutes. During this time gently embrace and caress each other.

2. Step back from under the shower head. Now M takes a bar of soap and vigorously massages R's entire body with it. Start by standing behind R and applying the soap to R's shoulders and back. Then kneel and attend to R's buttocks and the backs of R's legs. Next, R turns around, and M attends to the front of the body—first the neck, chest, and arms, then, while kneeling, the abdomen, legs, and genitals.

3. M and R reverse roles.

4. When both partners have been thoroughly soaped, step under the shower again, and rinse yourselves thoroughly.

5. M takes a palm leaf. Starting at R's neck, vigorously scrape the front of his or her body with the side of the leaf, continuing all the way to the genitals. (This is performed while you are standing under the shower spray.) Then, reaching behind R—with both arms around R's sides—vigorously scrape R's back with the palm leaf.

6. Reverse roles.

7. Lather and rinse each other again, as described above.

8. Leave the shower, and rub each other dry with Turkish towels.

Hot and Cold Towels

A favorite technique of Swedish masseurs and masseuses for facial massage is the hot towel.

Fold an ordinary Turkish towel in half lengthwise, then widthwise. Now dip it in a basin of scalding hot water, and wring it out.

Apply the towel to R's face, leaving only the nose exposed (so R can breathe). Press the towel gently against R's flesh, pushing in over the eyes, the cheeks, the temples, and other concave surfaces.

If the towel is too hot, unfold it, wave it once or twice in the air, then fold it again.

After R has been under the towel for two minutes, remove it, and perform facial massage. Then apply another hot towel for one to two minutes, followed by a cold towel for the same length of time.

If R has blackheads, the best time to squeeze them is after a hot towel. The cold towel then closes up the pores, keeping dirt out.

To round off the facial massage, apply some after-shave lotion or cologne. The effect is bracing.

Hot and cold towels may also be applied to the genitals. However, extremely hot towels should not be used. The temperature should be, at most, moderately hot.

Here is a genital massage technique involving hot and cold towels:

1. Dip a towel in hot water, then wring it out. Apply it to R's genitals pressing it against the organs. Leave it in place for about one minute.

2. With another towel wash the area surrounding the genitals—the abdomen, thighs, and buttocks. (The first towel remains in place while this is being done.) The washing motion should be firm but gentle. Soap is optional.

3. With the first towel wash the genitals.

4. Apply another hot towel to the genitals. Leave it in place for one minute.

5. Apply a cold towel. Leave it in place for one minute.

This technique is particularly effective in sexually arousing a man who is extremely tired or tense. It is less effective on women.

12

Massage
during Coitus

COMBINE the techniques of massage with the act of coitus, and you'll multiply the pleasures of sex tenfold.

Use the following suggested techniques as described, adapt them to your own tastes, or invent a few of your own.

Penile Massage during Coitus

While performing coitus in the conventional male-superior position (i.e., man on top, partners facing each other), the woman reaches behind her partner and places one or both hands between his thighs. In this position she has easy access to his scrotum, perineum, the base of his penis, and the lower portion of the penile stem.

To increase the sensations he enjoys during coitus, do one of the following:

1. Using the circular vibrating technique and two or three fingers, firmly massage the base of the penis.

2. Same as above, but also massage the perineum.

3. Take one testicle in each hand, and knead them gently.

4. Take the lower portion of the penile stem scissorslike between your index and middle fingers. Wiggle the fingers as quickly as possible.

5. Same as above, but with your other hand knead both testicles.

The above maneuvers may also be performed in other coital positions. In nonfacing positions the female gains access to the man's genitals by reaching between her own legs.

Massage of the Female Breasts and Genitals during Coitus

The male will have best access to the female breasts and genitals in rear-entry positions; he need only reach around his partner and touch these organs at will. In facing positions access will be slightly more difficult but by no means impossible.

Try the following techniques:

1. Take one breast in each hand; squeeze vigorously, caress gently, or perform gentle petrissage.

2. Roll R's nipples between your thumb and index finger.

3. Perform any of the other breast-stimulation techniques described in Chapter 6.

4. Using one or two fingers, gently perform the circular vibrating technique on the flesh that is covered by pubic hair.

5. Gently run your fingertips through the pubic hair.

6. Gently massage the pubic bone just above the clitoris.

7. Massage the clitoris itself and/or the area around it, using the techniques described in Chapter 6.

Anal and Other Extragenital Stimulation

Heighten the sensations of coitus by massaging the anal area, the thighs, the abdomen, and other parts of the body during coitus.

Massage of the anus and thighs can be particularly exciting. Employ the techniques described in Chapter 6. Remember, however, that some people have an aversion to anal stimulation and will be turned off by it.

Other SIGNET Titles of Special Interest

☐ **MAINLY FOR WIVES: The Art of Sex for Women by Robert Chartham.** An outspoken guide to the sex techniques that every woman should know to achieve a satisfying and mutually happy marriage. (#Q4884—95¢)

☐ **HUSBAND AND LOVER: The Art of Sex for Men by Robert Chartham.** A frank, authoritative guide describing in clear, everyday language the sex techniques every man should know in order to achieve a happy and satisfying marriage. (#Q4730—95¢)

☐ **SECRET AND FORBIDDEN by Paul Tabori.** A book that took ten years of research to complete, SECRET AND FORBIDDEN explores the erotic practices such as orgies, incest and homosexuality which have been banned by society for thousands of years. Richly illustrated, it is a bold and candid chronicle of vice through the centuries. (#Y4516—$1.25)

☐ **THE AFFAIR by Morton Hunt.** Explores one of the most engrossing and profoundly troubling of contemporary concerns. Morton Hunt allows readers to enter this secret underground world through actual words and experiences of eight unfaithful men and women. (#Y4548—$1.25)

☐ **AN ANALYSIS OF HUMAN SEXUAL INADEQUACY by Jhan and June Robbins.** A candid, accessible report on **Masters and Johnson's** Reproductive Biology Foundation. Described in laymen's terms and clinical detail, here are the step-by-step techniques used by Masters and Johnson to help the sexually troubled achieve adequacy and physical fulfillment. Included are articles by Margaret Mead and Rollo May. (#Q4445—95¢)

THE NEW AMERICAN LIBRARY, INC., P.O. Box 999, Bergenfield, New Jersey 07621

Please send me the SIGNET BOOKS I have checked above. I am enclosing $_____(check or money order — no currency or C.O.D.'s). Please include the list price plus 15¢ a copy to cover handling and mailing costs. (Prices and numbers are subject to change without notice.)

Address_____

City_____State_____Zip Code_____

Name_____

Allow at least 3 weeks for delivery

More SIGNET Titles of Special Interest

☐ **THE SEX RESEARCHERS by Edward M. Brecher.** The first historical account of Western Man's efforts to understand his own sexuality within a scientific framework from the secret sexual lives of the Victorians to the much publicized wife-swapping of the sixties. "Fascinating . . . belongs in most public and all college libraries." **Library Journal** (#W4518—$1.50)

☐ **UNDERSTANDING SEX: A Young Person's Guide by Dr. Alan F. Guttmacher.** A wholesome, clear and accurate explanation of human sexuality. Open, clear and frank, and directed to the questions of young people, it is the work of one of America's most distinguished physicians and author of the bestselling **Pregnancy and Birth.**
(#Q4349—95¢)

☐ **SEX BEFORE TWENTY by Helen Southard.** In this straightforward book, approved by the Child Study Association of America and adopted by the New York City Board of Education, a practicing psychologist talks honestly and realistically about the sexual questions that face young people today. (#T4636—75¢)

☐ **STUDENT GUIDE TO SEX ON CAMPUS by the Yale Committee on Human Sexuality.** This is the first sex manual written by college students, for college students and about college students. It doesn't preach, moralize or tell you how to behave. What it does do is tell you about birth control and answers questions most college students ask about sex. (#N4607—$1.00)